CLS COACHING ESSENTIALS

"A testimonial and instructional guide to help Coaches and Clients."

MICHELLE FRANKLIN

with Co-Authors Brianna Boomer, Chavon Thomas, Frances Ann Bailey, Marika Jankita, Marquita Daniel, Chanise L. Gilliam, Aleshia L.M. Brown, Carolyn Green

Unless otherwise noted, Scripture quotations are from the New King James Version of the Bible. Copyright 1979, 1980, 1982 by Thomas Nelson, Inc. Publishers.

Phoenix Publishing House, LLC
Publishers since 2016
P. O. BOX 154855
Lufkin, TX 75904

www.phoenixpubllc.com

Copyright ©2021 by Michelle Franklin.

All rights reserved. No part of this book may be reproduced, scanned, or distributed in any print or electronic form without permission. Please do not participate in or encourage piracy of copyrighted materials in violation of the author's rights. Purchase only authorized editions.

Printed in the United States of America

ISBN: 9798517701824

Table of Contents

1	**Life Coaching Program Outline**	7
2	**What is Life Coaching?**	12
3	**From the Counselor and Client's Corner**	17
4	**Making a Powershift in Your Coaching Business**	28
5	**Coaching Through Purpose in Position for Progress with Power**	37
6	**You Don't Have to Do It All**	44
7	**Fantabulous Pearls with Coach Chanise**	51
8	**Coaching from Behind the Chair**	59
9	**The Path of a Life Coach: The Ezekiel Method**	65
10	**Partnering to Fulfill Purpose**	75
11	**Questionnaire**	83

Life Coach Program Outline

"Learning how to coach others, through the process of life. While utilizing your life experience as a template."

Introduction

Michelle Franklin is the Founder of CLS Reflections Academy, Inc. CLS Reflections Academy is an institution established to help students implement morals, values, and create standards that will enhance spiritual, personal, and professional performance. With seventeen years in customer service, sixteen years in Ministry, ten years as a patient who battled multiple illnesses, and nineteen years of leadership experience, I came to notice a few very important components missing in the world and workforce; integrity, honesty, attentiveness, tenacity, competency, and common courtesy. Just to name a few.

Due to a lack of these qualities, organizations are being destroyed. If we don't shift our thinking, the legacy of many organizations, doesn't stand a chance. Through much research, I've discovered the missing component, Morality!

Morality is a particular system of values that are taught at home during the adolescent stages. Children are typically taught right from wrong to establish a pattern of positive behavior that benefit society as a whole. Due to broken homes and a lack of availability among parents, children are creating their own standards. Standards that are centered on self, instead of standards catered to selfless acts of kindness. CLS Academy's focus is to provide a course that focus on transformational leadership.

Transformational leadership's focus is to bring stabilization to the character of individuals. It challenges you to take ownership of your life through tasks that will enhance your day to day performance. Transformation is a renewing. You are taught to set structure, standards, and goals that will advance your life.

Developing character unlocks true potential and ignite a passion that pushes individuals to perfect themselves to perform better in their career choice. Parents and society, encourages students to pursue careers based on demand and financial stability. But, the purpose of character development is to discover who you are, and the purpose you're meant to serve. When purpose is revealed, it creates a passion that fuels creativity, momentum, and brings satisfaction to one's life.

Our ADS Model program builds character and provides a positive outlook on life for each student. It builds confidence, integrity, commitment, and most of all, awareness to strengths and weaknesses. We teach students how to navigate through hardship, tear down deficiencies, and resurrect character traits. Our company offers guaranteed improvement in personal & leadership development. I believe the reason many companies fold is not because of a lack of capital, but because of poor stewardship & poor personal performance. Poor personal performance is a result of poor character & leadership development. CLS development enhances customer services skills, and great customer service will increase your capital. Great stewardship strengthens your ability to manage capital, while leadership teaches you how to reinvest in it. If you want people to invest in your company's product & services, invest in your employees' growth & development.

CLS provides tools and techniques needed to coach clients into a secure career fueled by passions and persistence. Whether you're new to coaching or a seasoned professional looking for the next level, CLS will get you there. As a student exploring a new meaningful career path, by the time you graduate, you will have gained the information, techniques, and confidence to enhance every client you service.

CLS Reflection Academy assist with the development of the whole man while unlocking hidden potential, balance, and inner peace. Through our teaching, you'll learn the power of influencing the culture around you to lead, dominate, and transform your life and the life of others. We offer a variety of coaching programs.

What makes our school different is that we're not giving you something we've heard or read off of a paper. We're giving you life experience and coaching you through the process to becoming a Life Coach. We're not just giving you information, we're giving you a set of skills to enhance your life and the lives of your clients. The ADS Model of Coaching is an approach to bring alignment, demand, and stabilization.

Every program of this institution is a combination of Life Coaching and Specialty courses. It is based on our belief that every coach should adapt to the fundamentals of life skills before coaching others. Through observation, our institution makes sure each coach is well able and competent to function in the capacity of life and their Specialty. Life Coach is defined as a form of development in which a person, called a coach, supports their client in achieving a personal or professional goal. They offer training, wisdom, instruction, guidance, and help them make choices suitable for their future. Therefore, the coach must possess the capability to do so.

Alignment Demand Stabilization

This program is designed to keep you in alignment with your leadership goals and place a higher demand on you, while bringing stabilization to your gift. The implementation of this three part model creates a harmony within the spirit, soul, & body to bring a holistic approach to individualize the fullness of mankind. When each individual is properly aligned, it helps the body to grow, and build itself up. Making each human being distinct from their counterparts.
God created mankind authentic and to lead in their own capacity.

CLS Coaches and clients has teamed up to write this book to help encourage, empower, and equip anyone looking to become a coach. Whether you're a coach at CLS or from any other organization, you will be inspired by the testimonial and equipped with new strategies to help your clients.

What is Life Coaching?

Life Coaching is not just about partnering with your clients to help them in a thought provoking process, but it helps you to see if they're progressing or procrastinating. "You cannot be an Advocate from a broken place." Coaching provides a continuing support service.

You need to be a coach who understands the art of handling people in an open-minded manner. In short, the coach needs to be flexible enough to be able to earn the trust of the people being coached. The coach's style should enable a relationship of mutual respect as well as trust. The list below will help your clients understand the importance of coaching. Please explain every point to your clients.

- What is coaching going to achieve?
- It's important to have clear goals.
- Coaches identify needs and streamline issues in prevailing circumstances.
- A coach needs to be prepared for challenges.
- A coach needs to exercise patience.
- Identify standards and priorities.
- Connect them to their reality to face the truth.
- Establish new goals.
- Get them to commit.
- Identify and overcome obstacles.

- Assess and celebrate their successes.

Everything your clients do are habits they've grown accustomed to throughout the years. If they're functioning one way in a certain area, chances are they have been functioning that way in every area. Think about the way they pursue their process with you. If they don't submit to the process, it could be a sign of a lack of commitment, which could be the cause of their lack of productivity. Although they can advance in other areas, evaluating the process will reveal why they've put up a resistance in other areas. It's ok to have mercy and compassion. Sometimes people are they're own worst enemy. If you are a coach, follow the list below and take your clients through these steps. You'll see much growth.

Session one: Prioritize your areas of focus and evaluate which areas of your life that are bringing you satisfaction or dissatisfaction. Take time to write it down on paper. Habakkuk says to write the vision and make it plain. The goal is to use paper. Paper allows you to focus better on your weaknesses and strengths. It allows you to see the areas you need improvement in better. When on paper written with a pen, you can't erase it. The goal would be to use another piece of paper to track your progress. Based on this list, write down how people, places, things, and negative words play a part in your life/feelings and affects your daily life.

Session two: Write out a new standard for your life. One that's not easily broken. During this stage, you'll also write out new goals, make the proper adjustments and create a follow-through and follow-up plan. Doing this will reveal the areas you need improvements in. It'll also track your changes. The goal of coaching is to help you find your balance. Sometimes your family, friends, and career can get you off balance. The responsibility of a coach is to get you to cut back, eliminate, and try something new. You may have to move somethings and put people in a different place. Don't be stressed about it. You may have to be bold enough to rearrange them in your life. Instead of having them in your circle, move them to the middle or end section of your life. Follow the list below to see where you are in your life, or relationships.

- Which areas of my life are the most satisfying and fulfilling?
- In which area of my life am I feeling dissatisfied or unfulfilled?
- Which areas of my life could be even better?

Coaches use a solution-oriented method and aim to assist anyone who needs career advice or help accomplishing their goal. We help our clients to discover, redefine, and achieve their professional long and short-term goals and objectives. Coaches' tasks will always vary but, below is a list of tasks to help you get an idea of what's expected:

- Meeting with clients to learn their aspirations and goals.
- Identifying skills, difficulties, and opportunities and threats.
- Using tests to determine client's interests and skills.

- Assisting clients in finding opportunities through researching the markets.
- Giving tips and recommendations on how to keep going through adversity.
- Offering support and helping them work toward achieving a new mindset.
- Identifying clients' skills and helping them improve these skills and develop new ones.
- Facilitating conflict resolution.
- Tracking performance.
- Suggesting improvements to enhance.
- Discussing strategies to improve leadership, communication interpersonal skills, stress management, and self-confidence.
- Identifying the needs of their client and recommending assistance in those areas.
- Learn critical skills.
- Build confidence and know your value.
- Build new connections.
- Build confidence.
- Set goals and implement a roadmap to client's destination.
- People skills.
- Customer service skills.
- Goal setting.
- Following instructions.

Now that you've went over a few tips to help you become a better coach, let's begin reading our testimonials. At the end of each chapter, you'll find a place to take notes for yourself. Look to see what areas you can improve in and help others improve in. Take the test in the back to complete your process of improvement. Lastly, contact one of our coaches to book your appointment today!

Carolyn Collins-Green
From the Counselor and Client's Corner

From a client's perspective, I can share with you my belief that everybody needs someone to talk to. I can also share with you that we all have some type of issue, we all have had some type of matter in our lives, one way or another, that require us to search out Counselors for help. Some may need a counseling for one reason while others may need counseling for another. Proverb 15:22 says, "Without counsel purposes are disappointed but in the multitude of counselors, they are established." I never considered the works of a counselor until I sought out one to change my life. I am going to say, that if you do not find improvement in your life or situations after being counseled, the counselor you are seeing just may not be the counselor for you. Can I share my story?

When I first sought a counselor, I went to google seeking one. I submitted multiple surveys and assessments to be assigned to one that would be a match for me. I even thought I had found one and they took funds from my account but had not assigned anyone to me. I was so upset, I said to myself, "Just forget it." But then I went on social media and this young lady was presenting Chaplain Michelle as a good Spiritual Counselor.

So, reading this, the first thing I learned is that your counselor should be able to consult and counsel you in the way you are seeking help. I am a God-fearing person and love God. I have been put through the ringer in so many ways, so many times. I was angry and tired of being nice. I was ready to walk away from everything I knew in life. I just felt like I wanted to be by myself. Well, my spirit was pressed to give her a try. I called her and we talked before she confirmed she would counsel me. I say that because I have tried seeking other counseling resources, but time did not avail us. They were not exactly what I was seeking, or, on the other hand, I was not what they were willing to take on.

So, here, I decide to give Chaplain Michelle a call and she allowed me to just flow. She did not stop me at all, and I took full advantage of her courtesy. When I started feeling guilty of all I was pouring on her, she said to me, "I will counsel you," and then when she told me the cost I begin to cry again. So, I say this to share with others that what she showed me was compassion and concern for me.

From one phone call, she taught me that a Counselor should not just be interested in who they are or what they can do; they should first be concerned about the client. Truthfully, I know she knew that I was desperately seeking help and she could have charged me whatever and I would have paid. I instantly said thank you Jesus for sending her to me. The more we met, the better I felt. She was not just concerned about me, she was concerned about my health, wealth, my spiritual well-being, my soul, and my walk with Christ.

When I first begin counseling with Chaplain Michelle, I had no idea of who she was. As a prophet of God, she did not release her personal spiritual authority or position in ministry to me. I just knew her as Chaplain Michelle. So, there was no pressure about being confused on what to call her, how to speak to her, or what to say before her. She met me where I needed to be met. In the counseling and client's corner, a client should not be overwhelmed by position or power of a Counselor. Her approach gave me such an appreciation for who she was and how she does things. I am so grateful to God for my counselor.

Through God, I was led to her and I had come to believe that it was with divine purpose that we met. So now I am not just being mentally or physically counseled, but spiritually counseled as well. From my experience in the counselor and client's corner, I have learned that to be healed, it will take more than just treating the outward man. The inward man has to be treated just as well, if not more, for some of us. Are there counselors that will pray for you as well as treat your inner and outward being? A good counselor will do that for you. I encourage those who seek wholeness in their life to make sure that they pray before every decision, everything, and every matter, as well as pray afterwards.

In the counselor and client's corner, I can say that the experience has been life changing. Through her prayers, counseling, and mentoring, she has taught me so much. I have experienced deliverance like never before. She pushed me into a place of acceptance of myself. She challenged my ability to accept the truth about me! She challenged me not to revert to the negative thoughts or things that kept me in a place of bondage. From the client's corner, I learned that my state of being had nothing to do with those around me but everything to do with what I believed, thought about, and accepted.

Through our sessions, I learned that I was giving energy and power to the things I complained about, the things I feared coming upon me or my family. I had to stop saying yes to everything I feared and complained about and start declaring the promises of God, praying, and fix my mind to fight against the lies I was believing. ("So, a man thinks in his heart, so is he." -Proverbs 23:7)

She left her door open to me for any time, text, or call. She encouraged me not to hold my matters in or be secretive about things that stressed me, things I didn't understand, or things that brought out the worst in me. Whatever disturbed my peace, whatever intervened with God's will and way in my life, she expressed how I should give up control of the areas I felt were too hard for God. I was thinking as the world and not in faith. It was imperative that I fixed my mind and heart to align with the word of God spiritually. I had to change my ways, the way I thought, the way I was handling my matters, and change the way I was looking at life.

It was all about me. I was so busy trying to do it all on my own, Chaplain Michelle would never give me judgment or her personal take on matters. She just showed me how to look at a different pattern. I was given small assignments and tasks to do to defeat the mindset.

Do not conform to the pattern of this world but be transformed by the renewing of your mind. Then you will be able to test and approve what God's will is—his good,
pleasing and perfect will. Romans 12:2

There were times when I was given assignments and tasks to do to overcome and defeat the mindset that had held me bound for decades. One of my greatest assignments was she encouraged me to complete writing my book, *Lord! Teach Me To Fight!* I had shared with her that God had given me a book to write over a decade ago and I had not done so. She would encourage me to write the book. She explained that writing can be a healing method as well.
I knew that others would probably find healing in my story just as I may find healing in their stories. And they overcome him by the blood of the lamb and the word of their testimony; and they loved not their lives unto death (Revelation 12:11). From the client's corner, this taught me that sometimes our healing and deliverance is tied to the release of our story.

In one of my counseling sessions, there was a discussion opened up that was tied to my deliverance from a very difficult experience I had. I guess it was so severe to me that I had suppressed it. As we begin my session the conversation led Chaplain Michelle to share with me a personal experience she had, and it hit me like a ton of bricks. I was so resentful, hurt, and angry to remember the experience that I was crying and devastated. I had not discussed this with her, and it was because I didn't want to remember it. It was one of the most difficult times in my life. But, in her sharing her testimony I had a breakthrough and was delivered from that hurt, anger, and resentment. It seemed as if every time we met, my life was in a better place. My family was in a better place. My rest had been better, my mind has been better, and most of all, my spiritual walk has been better.

As a client under the coaching of Author Michelle Franklin and being led by her in her obedience to God, I have learned that we all are capable of delivering, activating, and releasing one another to bring healing and strength forward. I learned this through my experience as a client under her leadership. For more than two decades, I had been trapped in my own mind. Held bound by the things I had not repented to God. So, you know how people look at your outward appearance and determine that you are a strong, God-fearing woman? Little did they know, I hated myself. I hated the corporate that caused me the pain and suffering.

While I was being taught, I was still leading others, delivering others, activating others, and releasing others. Her teaching enabled me to teach those who were before me. I am better because of my confessions and repentance. I am able to confess and repent because of her obedience to God. God requires us to be obedient to what we have been called to do. We all overcome by the blood of Jesus Christ and the word of our testimony. We give one another knowledge when we open our mouths.

The one person closest to me that should have protected me and provided for me was trying to destroy me. Trying to fight in my own strength and power drained me. It consumed me of who I was to be and what I should have been doing in the Kingdom of God. I was tormented by the trickery of the enemy.

I was helping the enemy torment me. I was in no way guilty of anything yet, I was because I had not fully forgiven, repented, and walked in Christ Jesus as I should have.

But now, I know better because of the client's corner, I have activated my ability to fight. I know spiritually that the weapons of my warfare are not carnal but mighty through God, through the pulling down of strongholds. I am not consumed by the attacks as I was prior to my visiting the client's corner. I had to sit at the feet of the teacher and humble myself, admit to myself, commit to myself, and love myself. However, little did I know, that there was unseen trickery at work with me. Me, a person who was considered one of God's faithful servants.

I was the one people have been confirming of the change they see in me since I have been in the client's corner. I was backed into a corner. Bent down into a corner as a little girl. But now! That little girl has been released and she is now more developed, more stronger, and more wiser.

The client corner is a place of deliverance, a place of activation, and a place of release. I have always been a woman of God. I have always been a servant of God. I have always loved God and His people, but there was so much in me that needed to be released, and some things that still does. Deliverance is an ongoing need for all of us. However, now that I have been released from a lot of things in my life; I have been transformed. The proof is not just my word of testimony, but my family, friends, and others. My appearance has changed, my conversation has changed, my confidence has changed, my appearance has changed. The enemy has to rethink his game when it comes to attacking me. Through the Counselor and client's corner, I have learned to fight! God is awesome in what He does, let Him work.

He will give you what you need, when you need it, and how you need it. He knew that I needed the Counselor that was sent in my life, and now that I have grown so much mor., I go boldly through the Throne of Grace and I go gratefully to the Counselor and client's corner when I need to. Though I continue to be taught, I am well-trained by the word and work of God through the woman of God. Thank you, Author Michelle Franklin, for being a vessel.

My counselor is always asking me, "Are you OK? Do we need to meet?" Sometimes I tell her, "No, we are good. Go ahead and handle your business." She is a very busy soldier. You know how when the counseling experience is going so well that you feel like you are not in need of the meetings so frequently, but you're not ready to let go of them? I feel it approaching, and I feel like it is nearing. But I am glad that God is healing me through her Counseling and has called me to be assigned under her leadership. She is an awesome counselor and woman of God.

How can I become better at what I do?

Frances Bailey Chapter
Making a Powershift in Your Coaching Business

After overcoming everything that was meant to destroy me, I decided to use my authentic voice to help others overcome obstacles and opportunities sent their way to stop them by birthing my coaching business. I use my experiences and Godly wisdom to help direct others on a path to recover and succeed. Even though, I had a great vision for helping others, there were some things I had to do in order to see my coaching business excel and become impactful. Some important things that I did were:

1. **Pick the Vision Up and Implement**

A lot of times we have the vision and dream to launch our coaching business but somewhere along the line we put it back down. Some things come up, we feel the time isn't right or fear begins to creep in the unknown. I had to realize that my vision was a desire of my heart that Christ had given me, and I couldn't sit and allow that to remain dormant.

I had to push away the distractions and pick it back up and then do my part to implement it. The implementation part required three important F's. I wasn't waiting on God anymore; God was waiting on me to obey and launch. I had to move prophetically with no fear, having faith, and remaining faithful. I had to keep these three things in mind throughout my whole coaching journey, remembering that God wouldn't be asking me to do anything that he wouldn't give me the strength for or equip me for, so why fear? I also knew that even if I felt a little scared or uncomfortable during this process, I had to still do it, even if I did it scared. You only fail when you never take action. Things also came during my process, but I had to remain faithful to what God had called me to do. Faithful did not mean I had to be perfect, I just chose to remain steadfast in my calling.

2. **Have a Blueprint and Motive to be Intentional**

Once I knew that I had to pick the vison up and go forth. I began to lay out a strategic plan in pursuing my goal of a coaching business. Your blueprint should include steps needed to become certified, some branding, and your motive.

I enrolled in a course that gave me several coaching certifications for the areas that I wanted to target. I had to become clear on who exactly I was trying to reach in order to be intentional and effective in my coaching business. Knowing my why also helped to have a clear blueprint and to stay grounded in my plan. When you know who you are trying to reach and why, it makes the process a lot easier and eliminates unnecessary confusion when trying to attract clients and engage in your target audience. Checking your motive is also important when laying out any agenda. You should ensure that your motive is pure. Hidden agendas, launching from a place of rejection, hurt, comparison, etc... could all be aspects to not only cause your business not to grow but also, to be draining. When you coach, you should coach from a place of pureness and wholeness. One important tip is to never minister from a place of brokenness. Ensure you aren't speaking from a place anger or vengeance to your client.

3. Collaborate, Network, Gain Midwives

Never be afraid to ask for help or guidance. During this process, it is important to be around those who can encourage you, add to you, push you, and those that can hold you up. That's why I had a midwife during the launching of my business.

I couldn't afford to be around the naysayers, the doubters, or those who didn't understand the vision God had given me. Furthermore, I have had to seek guidance and wisdom from those who are already where I wanted to be in business. I collaborated with some of their programs and in the process, learned the ins and outs of how a coaching business worked. I gained some crucial information by getting uncomfortable and networking with complete strangers who began to pour into the things that helped to shift my business. By stepping outside of my comfort zone, I gained connections that were international which led to my business achieving an international status before it hit the year anniversary. It is important to connect with those where you are trying to go and then prepare for where you are about to go. Working together with others also helped to shift my coaching business.

Collaborating with others gives you the opportunity to reach even more of your audience. There is power and favor connected to networking and collaborating. Don't miss your opportunity competing with others that you become too prideful to ask for guidance. Networking, Collaborating, and Midwives shifted my business into greatness.

4. **Have a Value Closer**

In your coaching business, you should be able to say why your business gives value with their investment. Some clients are not anxious to invest in your sessions if they don't see where you could add value to them. I made sure to point out three important value closers that my clients could expect to receive when working with me. Some examples of value closers are: mindset transformations, accountability, and strategic plan layouts. I let my clients know that we believe who we are by whatever is in our heart. The heart and the mind work interchangeably so I work to help transform the heart so that it flows positive attributes to the mind. Then the positive that is in the mind manifests within your life. Your mindset (heart) is your power.

Accountability helps clients to realize that they are their biggest enemy. Nothing or no one can stop them. Accountability isn't condemnation but inspiration to realize what you could do differently to accomplish, heal, and overcome barriers. I hold follow-up calls and bookings after some services are provided. My clients connect with me more intimately and don't just feel like a paying client.

5. Submit Your Will, Mission, and Gift unto Christ

To gain true success is to first submit your goals, plans, and visons to Him first. Acknowledge Him in all that you do, then execute the plan. The best way is to do it Gods way. By submitting your will to His, you are trusting God to keep in His will for your life. During your journey of coaching, there may be some things that you may want to do that aren't wrong, it's just that it may not line up with the purpose God has called you for and to reach the people he wants you to reach. These things can become distractions, putting you off the path you are supposed to be on.

Submitting your mission, goals, vision, and gift to God, allows him to do the exalting and elevating of your business when it's time.

You can trust him to direct your path to reap a harvest of positive fruit. Submitting to him is the root of the powershift you are looking for in your business. Having and growing an effective and impactful coaching business starts with you. There are so many different things you could do to cause a powershift in your coaching business and your mentorships, but these were some important characteristics that really helped my business to flourish. Every day in your business you will learn more effective things if you continue to be a student while being a coach.

Never stop learning and implementing. Taking action and keeping your momentum is the key to any type of powershift. You may slow down but, don't take your foot off the pedal. Keep looking for new ways and new connections to grow your business.

Contact Information:

Personal Facebook
Page: https://www.facebook.com/frances.collins.7

Twitter: https://www.twitter.com/FranAnnBailey

Instagram: https://www.Instagram.com/FranAnnBailey

Frances Bailey Enterprises Business
Page: https://www.facebook.com/PurposeZeal/

Frances Author Page: https://www.facebook.com/FranAnnBailey/

Linkedin: http://linkedin.com/in/franannbailey

Clubhouse: @FranAnnBailey

Website: www.francesannbailey.com

Podcast: Purpose Is Greater

How can I become better at what I do?

Brianna Boomer (Brianna B)
Coaching Through Purpose in Position For Progress with Power

Coaching Through Purpose

We were all born on purpose for a purpose. Despite how the story goes, we are alive and called to use what God has placed inside of us to better the land. Being a coach is more than just helping others. You are pushing people to walk in their purpose through discovering their calling and leading them step-by-step through this journey called life. With the ups and downs of being the coach or the client, we all have a purpose. Definition being "the reason that something is done or created or for which something exists" (oxford language). To break that down, "reason" you have to have a "why". Why do you what to be a coach? Why do you want to help people make progress? Why do you want to be that person that holds the title of accountability for people you barely know? This may seem simple, but it is very important. There will be days where you want to quit, you want to throw in the towel and say forget everybody and their goals, but your WHY will remind you of your calling, your purpose, and why you choose to take on the role of coach in a world of 8 billion humans. "Created." God wanted and made you to be the very person you are today; the help, the motivator, the encourager, the strategist, and above a servant to guide the lost. "Exist." This is why you are alive, this very profession helps you to survive knowing what you do and the affect it has on others. Being a good effective life coach is a gift. Appreciate it, accept it, grow in it, and use it to make the world a better place one person at a time.

Coaching in Position

When I refer to position, I mean being in the right place in your life to coach others. I am not saying you must be perfect or have yourself all together. No, that's a big misunderstanding when it comes to helping others. However, you do have to be in a healthy place where you are not pushing off your own hurt and traumatic advice on others. When people go through personal situations in life or simply just trying to find their way, they cannot give their 100% best effort to their clients. Being a coach gets pushed to the back of their focus and their clients are left without guidance, accountably, and someone to believe in them. So instead of them being the only one going through, now innocent people are caught in the mist of chaos. When I first started out coaching, I was young, liked helping others, and wanted to make extra income. On top of all of that, I was in college and working full time. Yes, I had a lot going on, so my clients, aka, the 3 people that believed in me, didn't get the best of me because I was so stretched out doing everything else trying to find my way. I was in no place to effectively help others because I was constantly thinking about how I could get ahead and better my own life.

Needless to say, my clients didn't do so well either due to me not being able pour into them fully. So that saying, "you can't pour from an empty cup," is so true. We must take care of ourselves. Make sure our cup is full and ready to run over because what is in the cup is for you, everything that overflows is for other people. In order to be effective and really make a difference in the world we must show up for ourselves, our families, clients, and those we encounter every day. If you do run into circumstance where we need to take a step back, IT IS OKAY. Be honest with yourself and your clients if you need to take some time. During these times I have set activities/objectives in place to send to clients to keep them moving forward. Whether it be, an *How You Feel* assessment or journal prompt. I have these in my just-in-case folder. So every day, ask yourself if you are in a good position to be there for someone else. The answer will determine how your day/session will go.

Coaching for Progress

IT IS NOT AN OVERNIGHT PROCESS. Keep this in mind when you are working with someone who is not progressing yet or as fast as you would like. Some clients can take from 3 days to 3 years to accomplish one simple (what we may think is simple may not be for them) task. Keep in mind that we coach for progression not for perfection. Be firm, however, let them work at their pace. If they channel how accomplishment and success feels then they will begin to accelerate into whatever they choose. Our job is to help clarify the vision and provide strategy to take them to the next level and accountability to keep going. Do not take it personal or like you are not doing enough when things get slow. If your client is still making some progress, even if it's small, then you are still doing your part. Some people do need that extra push, and some will begin to separate and push you away if pushed too hard. You must know who you are dealing with and learn their way of moving forward. It's not the same for everybody because of the background differences. So, in the beginning, get to know your clients, their desires, what motivated them, their triggers, their interests, and dislikes. When you build the rapport then it will be easier to channel what you bring to the table and what they can use to help, then progress in certain or all aspects of their life. There will be times where your clients start to regress and this is when you really have to take a step back, analyze, and ask do they need more then you can give. You are not a therapist or counselor, so it's important to know when it's time to refer them to seek deeper help. That is still progress. Know that they will get the help they need and be able to handle situations and development skills to go along with coaching to enhance results.

Coaching with Power

Use you gifts and the special abilities that only you have to make your coaching unique to you. You can only give what you have. Often times we don't realize what we are capable of until we have no other choice but to rely on just that. There are millions of life coaches in the world, but there is only one you. Which means only you can do it how you do it. Don't be discouraged about other coaches. They have their superpower and you do too. Once we learn our abilities and what we specialize in, that sparks coaching confidence. Tapping into everything we do with power. Using what you have and the resources available at your full advantage to help better yourself and excel at assisting your clients transform their own life. This same power will rub off on your clients if they see you fully walking boldly into what you do without doubt or fear. Yes, you will have some down times. Yes, you will have rough days. Yes, there will be times where you feel like you don't have what it takes, but those are the times you use your inner power to push through. No superhero was ever down for long. Remember, you can be down but don't let that defeat you and your purpose to change people's lives. It's bigger than you. When you help one succeed, you are not just helping turn dreams into reality but you helping families live abundantly; a business thrives, a legacy to be left for the next generation. If that's not a superpower then I don't know what is. Stay encouraged along the journey and always remember your power.

Contact Information:

Better Becomings LLC (Facebook Page)
BetterBecomings.com
757-559-1584
Betterbecomings@gmail.com
Briannab_live (Instagram)

How can I become better at what I do?

Marika Hunt
You Don't Have To Do It All
Coaching to Leadership

Being a great leader is not about thinking you know everything, or able to do it all. It's about realizing that in your weakness you are made strong with the team you build to help carry out the daily task. It takes a level of humility to recognize that you need help to advance the kingdom, business, or any organization. As a leader, the foundation, which is your team, should be built with a clear understanding of what you're expecting. It will require communication skills and a level of emotional intelligence to be able to handle conflict as well.

One great quality of leadership is the ability to delegate, which frees you up to focus on other duties, which offers time efficiency, that we are being productive and utilizing our time wisely. Delegation creates a sense of trust with the team, and it also gives others the ability to discover a skill set they didn't know they had or to learn something new to enhance your cognitive functions. A great example of this leadership ability being displayed is Moses with counsel from his father-in-law Jethro in the book of Exodus 18.

The first thing in Exodus Chapter 18:7-9, was Moses bowing downing, and kissed his father-in-law. So the first thing in delegating as a leader is, can you honor others and receive counsel from those closes to you? Can you receive the counsel even when your rank in spirit or the natural is higher than theirs? Or, will you reject it because you think they don't rank enough to even come to you? As a leader, you have to be open to not only giving counsel but also being okay receiving counsel as well. Who knows us better than those we communion with daily? Those closest to us can see us better than we can see ourselves at times, and when you're vulnerable to receive counsel, it leaves less room for error.

Jethro, in verse 14, sees all that Moses is doing for people as a judge from morning to evening. Jethro is concerned and tells Moses in verse 18 that this will surely wear him and the people with him out. This is another reason why delegation is important because if you don't prioritize responsibility among others it can physically and emotionally drain you. Then other high-level tasks you should be focused on will get put on the back burner and can be detrimental to your ministry, business, or organization. I've seen some great leaders leave this earth prematurely because they were trying to do it all when none of us have the capacity to do it. Jesus could have done it all but even he chose 12 disciples to help him carry out the mission for the Kingdom of God.

Another key factor in delegation, is creating strategies just like Jethro did for Moses concerning how to carry out his Kingdom assignment. Having strategy helps you to have a solid foundation to build on and less room for error. Strategies also provide the team with a vision, so they will know the objective goals that you're trying to obtain. Then it also establishes structure for the team, so that everyone knows their role and doesn't try to do a role they weren't assigned. Strategies and structure is very important because when there are guidelines into play, there is no confusion on what needs to be done, what everyone's tasks are, and the expectation on when those task need to be executed.

A second key factor in leadership would be to focus on training and teaching. Just as Jethro was instructed in Exodus 18:20. As a leader you can't expect them to carry out a task they have never been trained in or received the wisdom and knowledge to carry it out. This also comes with you knowing their limitations as well. You don't want something in their hands that they don't have the capacity to carry out. As the leader, you should be able to teach them the word and be an example on how to live out what you put out of your mouth. Teaching them the words displays what God is expecting from them as they go forth in power and authority. A third key factor in delegation, is the discerning of spirits. When you're able to determine what is good and evil, and distinguish what spirit is in operation.

In verse 21, Moses had to select men who were competent and feared God; men of truth, those who hate dishonest gain. This could not have been done if Moses' vison was distorted by anything outside of God. If your picking mechanism is off, then you're liable to select people who may be some stiff necks, impure motives, unstable in all of their ways, and blows with every wind that comes. There is a sense of relief when you have a team you can trust with the vision and can assist you in carrying out God's assignments concerning building the Kingdom.

A fourth key factor in delegation, is a leader must know how to handle conflict, just as the team should. In verse 22, one of their tasks was to be able to handle conflict to take some of the load off of Moses. This will require the team to decipher what conflicts goes to their leader and what they can handle on their own. A level of maturity and the ability to control your own emotions is necessary when dealing with conflict. If not, then someone else's conflict could very well reveal what's not dead in you. We are not able to deal with what we haven't mastered ourselves. So, handling conflict will require you to crucify your own flesh daily so that the decisions you make in a situation is right in the eyesight of God, and not what you think is right.

A fifth key factor in delegation, is a leader must have an ear to listen. In verse 24, Moses executed everything his father-in-law said. Moses, being open to receive counsel, enhanced the structure of the leadership team which allowed him to choose able men from all of Israel and made them heads over people, leaders of thousands, of hundreds, of fifties, and of tens {from the highest to the lowest judicial levels}. Moses willingness to position the able men set order among Israel.

Delegation, as you can see, is very necessary in leadership, Moses' listening allowed him to realize he needed help to properly lead the people. When releasing responsibility to your team, it builds a sense of trust. Even when you're not around, things will still get accomplished. This will also reveal to you who is ready for more responsibility in the time they take to get things done, how well they do it in excellence, and how well they know you.

Contact Information:

Marika J/Marika Hightower
Marika J ministries on FB
Marika Jankita on FB
marikaj2020@gmail.com

How can I become better at what I do?

Coach Chanise Gilliam

Fantabulous Pearls with Coach Chanise

Foundational Fantabulous Pearls for Your Success

We all have dreams and goals in our hearts that we have started and stopped. It's not that we are not capable. Most times it's because there is not a clear plan or intention toward those dreams and goals. In my own personal journey, I started and stopped so many times fully knowing that I had what it took to accomplish what was in my heart. I was missing foundational tools to sustain me on my path to success. What you see today is the fruit of what started on the inside. The following Fantabulous Pearls are foundational tools that are worked together throughout your journey. The Breath of Recovery, close your eyes and see, and taking intentional steps one at a time.

The Breath of Recovery

Breathe in, breathe out. It's such a natural and simple thing to do that is often taken for granted. Yet, it is the most powerful and cleansing gift from God. God created our bodies fearfully and wonderfully to heal and rejuvenate itself.

To intentionally inhale and exhale is one of the first things that I do when I am feeling tired, overwhelmed, nervous, frustrated... should I go on? This is called **The Breath of Recovery.** I can best describe Breath of Recovery as releasing the weighted layers of life and recovering the power, love, and a sound mind.

We must always know the source of our breath and the benefits of that breath. Genesis 2:7 describes how *the LORD God formed man of the dust of the ground, and breathed into his nostrils the breath of life; and man became a living soul.* I would go as far to say, "That Breath" is both natural and spiritual. There is a recovery that happens when we breathe with intention. When you are feeling any type of emotions that are pulling you in a place of disempowerment, recover the power of The Breath inside of you. Inhale power, love, and the sound mind that God has given you. Exhale the fear, doubt, and unbelief that creeps in through the weight and layers of life. Now you are ready to say who you are with the breath you have recovered. Silence the negative self-talk and thoughts by using the breath you recovered to tell yourself audibly who you are. We can not speak to yourself without taking a breath. Recover your energy by saying, "I am energized for this task." Instead of saying, "I'm tired." Recover your time by saying, "I manage myself well with the time that I have." Instead of saying, "I am so busy, I can't get anything done." If you say these things to yourself, while intentionally breathing in and breathing out, you will experience inner strength and stamina for the journey.

Recover who you are designed and created to be with every intentional breath.

Close Your Eyes and See

As you are releasing the weight of life through Recovery Breathing and using your God given breath to tell yourself who you are, **close your eyes and see.** Close your eyes and see yourself being more than a conqueror and well-able to do all things through Christ gives you strength (Romans 8:37 and Philippians 3:13). Take your power back and do not allow your sight to cloud your vision. See yourself being successful in your purpose. See yourself pressing through challenges. See you're healed from the wounds of life that have anchored you to only get so far. Most importantly, see yourself NOW. See the value, see where adjustments need to be made, and see your growth.

Then you must continue to breathe and say what you see. You can also keep a journal of what you are seeing. You will not get to where you are created to be until you see yourself now and see yourself there. Even though you may see it, "How" you get "there" is not all mapped out. It is a windy road of valuable Fantabulous Pearls that you will be able to add to your tool box of life. When you see beyond being overwhelmed with a task, you see micro strategies to accomplish a macro task.

Seeing beyond fear empowers you to see yourself in motion growing stronger and better each day. Take a few moments right now and just…. breathe as you close your eyes and see.

Intentionally Take One Day At A Time

You may ask, what do I do with what I am seeing? What do I do with what seems so far out of reach? Take the next step with your journal and see it as a financial leger that keeps track of what adds value to you and what has decreased your value. It's ok to identify those things that have chipped away at your worth because it puts you in the place of awareness. Once you are aware of what is taking away from you, you can give yourself permission to see yourself beyond where you are, write it down, and take one day at a time toward what you see. That first step may seem scary or you may not even know what step to take. The book of wisdom in Proverbs 19:20-21 instructs us to:

Listen to counsel and receive instruction, That you may be wise in your latter days. There are many plans in a man's heart, Nevertheless the Lord's counsel—that will stand.

In my personal experience, the Lord used people to counsel me how to <u>practically</u> walk out what I was seeing. It's not out of your reach, it's within you. You are fully loaded with everything you need to be. It's not about what you do, it's who you are. Out of this place of "being" you, "do" one step at a time. Everything we do in life is a process. When we get up in the morning, there is a process or routine that we go through to get ready for our day.

When you clean a kitchen, there is a process. In the process, there are steps and those steps are taking one step at a time until it is completed. We must look at our goals and the processes as a journey. Research the journey, plan the journey, and prepare for the journey one intentional step at a time. If you go on a trip, we take intentional steps to prepare to arrive "there". Where, When, Why, What, and How is gathered and put into place one step at a time. Some would even go to the lengths to talk with someone who has been where they plan to travel. Why would we do any less when it comes to our purpose and destiny? Unfortunately, we do not always put intentionally in the steps of our process. Nevertheless, the same intentional steps toward your goals will make big changes over time.

My husband and I were having a conversation about our future and he said we must "get ready to be ready". There was such a vector of "Wowness" in the statement. When we empower ourselves through the breath of recovery, closing our eyes and seeing, then taking one intentional step at a time, we set ourselves on a solid path of success. Through the hills, valleys, bumps, and victories in our process, there is so much to gain. It's for our making, molding, testing, and proving. There is a process that must take place in our preparation for opportunities that are designed for us. It's time to get ready to be ready for success by applying these Fantabulous Pearls.

Contact Information:

Coach Chanise Gilliam 503-473-6751

LadyChanise@gmail.com

Facebook https://www.facebook.com/CoachChanise

IG Fantabulous Pearls.

How can I become better at what I do?

Marquita Daniel
Coaching From Behind The Chair

Ten years ago, if you would've told me that I'd be a Hairstylist, let alone a Certified Trichologist and owner of a beauty and wellness center, I would have laughed. The truth of the matter is, I knew nothing about hair, and actually always wanted to do social work. Now look here, 8 years later, I am a Certified Life & Empowerment Coach. God has a funny way of bringing things full circle. You see, growing up I thought hairstylists were born with this talent. It seemed like everyone I came across had been doing hair since the age of 5 years old. Me, on the other hand, I was 28 years old and knew absolutely nothing about hair. All I knew is that I heard God say, "Do it" and I did. To be honest, that was the second best decision I've made in my life.

Throughout this journey one of the most vital things I've learned is the importance of personal development. Coming into this industry, I thought it was all about delivering beautiful hairstyles and great customer service. Oh, boy, was I wrong! The reality of it is that, it's much deeper than hair. Being in the beauty industry, you will come across a little bit of everything. Whether it's clients dealing with relationship issues, self-esteem, family disputes, health challenges, or even something as simple as a tough day at work, we must be equipped and whole to handle these situations.

When coaching from behind the chair, it is important that we maintain a safe space for our clients. Our atmosphere plays an important part in this. Creating a conducive atmosphere in your salon is very important. When a client walks into your establishment, they should feel peace and comfort. Also, it is so crucial that we maintain a high level of integrity and confidentiality. Our clients should feel comfortable with opening up and sharing, while knowing that their business will never leave that conversation. We must build trust and in order to handle these situations we must be healed and whole ourselves, or at least actively working towards it. Here are examples of some personal experiences I've had with coaching from behind the chair:

Client #1 "I Am Not Worthy."

There was a young lady in her early 20's who frequently came into the salon for services. I noticed early on that whenever I gave this client compliments, she would always put her head down and rebuttal with a negative comment about herself. When I noticed this, I became intentional about speaking life into her and pointing out the amazing things about her. She eventually opened up and shared some challenges she had with loving and believing in herself, which stemmed from childhood rejection. She then said that because of the positive words and encouragement she receives at her appointments, she's starting to look at herself differently and she's now motivated to work towards some goals that she has.

Our words have power and carries weight. Words of affirmation can go a long way.

Client #2 "I'm Not Sure If God Loves Me."

A new client came in for services. We spent time talking about her commute to the salon and who referred her to me. She then shared that she just had a baby and that it was tough. She opened up and shared that she's still trying to find her way. I then heard God tell me to give her a little of my story. I began tell her a little about my story. She began to weep and shared some things she went through in her life. Those things were very traumatic and made her question if God even loved her. Me, sharing my story with her, was a faith builder for her and gave her hope to keep pushing.
This, also, was a lesson for me. DO NOT BE ASHAMED OF YOUR STORY. It could really bless someone.

Client #3 "I Don't Want To Live."

Remember, I told you how important it was to create an atmosphere conducive for the Holy Spirit to move? Let me give you an example. A client came in for services, and I sensed a heaviness on her. My first thought was to continue to spark conversation and maybe that would help her. I, then, heard God say to turn a specific song on. Midway through the song, she jumped out the chair and began to scream and praise God. I, then, started praying and speaking life into her, which turned into a full-blown deliverance session.

She later shared that she wanted to take her own life, but something broke when she came into the salon. Never underestimate where God can move.

Coaching from behind the chair not only requires relationship and trust building, but it also requires obedience. Being obedient to the voice of God will allow you, to not only give the clients what they want, but you'll also give them what they need.

Contact Information:

Facebook.com/marquitadaniel1
IG @itsmarquitadaniel
Marquitadaniel.com

How can I become better at what I do?

Aleshia Brown
The Path of a Life Coach: The Ezekiel Method

Proverbs 15:4 – *A gentle tongue is a tree of life, but perverseness breaks the spirit.*

The power is in your tongue. You can choose to speak life or death. *From the fruit of a man's mouth, his stomach is satisfied; he is satisfied by the yield of his lips. Death and life are in the power of the tongue, and those who love it will eat its fruits* (Proverbs 18:20-21). When you embark on the path of becoming a life coach, you have made a conscious decision to speak life into the areas of others that feel dormant and dead. At times they may feel lost, abandoned, and with no sense of direction.

The purpose of a life coach is to help one find direction, peace, hope, joy, and a secure sovereign place within themselves. At times we look for things that we already have within us, feelbut they may have been buried by the trials, tribulations, negativity, lies, and the way of life's obstacles. It's hard for one to find them truly. It can become challenging for someone to believe again, yet dream, when it appears that all they face is bumping into walls, feeling caved in, and like a constant failure. These feelings can cause someone to feel lifeless, and it is as if they have died and need to be revived again.

A life coach acts as a defibrillator. The words that come out of one's mouth send an electrical shock to the heart, mind, body, and soul; stimulating and reviving those things that are dead within someone. It is important as a life coach to be mindful of your words because they hold weight and power. *The words of a man's mouth are deep waters; the fountain of wisdom is a bubbling brook. Gracious words are like a honeycomb, sweetness to the soul and health to the body. Let no corrupting talk come out of your mouths, but only such as is good for building up, as fits the occasion, that it may give grace to those who hear. Let your speech always be gracious, seasoned with salt, so that you may know how you ought to answer each person* (Proverbs 18:4, 16:24, Ephesians 4:29, Colossians 4:6). One must be in the position to speak words of affirmation, reassurance, confirmation, and life.

Being a life coach also requires the skill of actively listening. Actively listening and discernment give way to discover those dead places. An investigator can only solve the mystery if they actively listen to those in question and use their insight to detect the truth from a lie and discover any unknown clues that will help solve it. God created us with one mouth and two ears for a reason. *Know this, my beloved brothers: let every person be quick to hear, slow to speak, slow to anger. He who has ears to hear, let him hear* (James 1:19, Matthew 11:15).

It is not always that a life coach must talk but do more listening than anything. By increasing the skill of actively listening, it places one in the position to better develop an action plan that is best suited for the client. Not every client will be the same, some need the actions of both the mouth and the ears, and some require a listening ear to talk out their thoughts. In their talking, they discover a more profound revelation and solution to their concerns and feelings and be provided a sense of reassurance that they are on the right path.

The Ezekiel Method

In the book of Ezekiel, the thirty-seventh chapter, God poses a question, "Do you think these dry bones can live?" It is not that God did not know the answer to the question being asked; God utilized this method to stimulate the mind of Ezekiel and discover his way of thinking. As life coaches, we can ask questions to help clients find solutions and face their inner truths/beliefs. *You have not because you ask not* (James 4:2). For one to break a habit, one must first discover the pattern. Learning the pattern comes through the life coach asking questions that the client in turn answers.

Once God asked Ezekiel a general question, Ezekiel's response was, "Sovereign Lord, you alone know" (Ezekiel 37:3). God knew that the bones could live, but God wanted to know he believed this same thing. When asking your client questions (investigating), your discernment has already given you the answers to these questions. Still, you want to get the client to stimulate their mind by profoundly thinking about the answers to every question.

This exercise works the brain to think and allows the client to hear out loud the thoughts from within their brain. When detoxing and restructuring the brain from negative thoughts, one must speak, releasing every feeling that they might have.

The body was created to naturally eliminate any foreign substances that do not belong through bowel movements, vomiting, etc. When the client begins to speak out loud their toxic inner thoughts, it is as if they are vomiting out the toxins within their brains. Ezekiel's response gave God a sense of direction and revealed to God his current mindset and way of thinking, and allowed him to eliminate the toxins. With this discovery, God then gives him some instructions and an assignment to complete. This assignment now stimulates the mind differently by replacing the toxins with nutrition (positive actions/words).

The instructions were broken down into stages/steps. The first step was, *Prophesy to these bones and say to them, 'Dry bones, hear the word of the Lord!' This is what the Sovereign Lord says to these bones: I will make breath[a] enter you, and you will come to life. I will attach tendons to you and make flesh come upon you and cover you with skin; I will put breath in you, and you will come to life. Then you will know that I am the Lord* (Ezekiel 37:4-6).

After completing the first step, he began to see results which gave him the momentum to keep going. The next step was, *Prophesy to the breath; prophesy, son of man, and say to it, 'This is what the Sovereign Lord says: Come, breath, from the four winds and breathe into these slain, that they may live'* (Ezekiel 37:9).

After completing this step, he saw even more significant results, which built his confidence even more. Once the activity was completed, God then explained to him the purpose of the action and all that it resembled. At times your clients will be so buried with life's struggles, it is hard for them to see anything positive or more significant. The importance of assignments and activities is getting the client involved, having them do things they never thought they could do. Also, it is in the results. Once the tasks and activities are completed, if the client sees results and a positive change within themselves, it will motivate them to want to do more, and want to continue. This is a part of building their self-esteem back up and their motivation to dream and hope again by giving them back the feeling of I CAN! Through the instructions and the voice of belief, it gave Ezekiel momentum to go forth and begin to speak life. The purpose of a life coach is to bring to life the reality of the choices made in one's life. Through questionnaires and active listening helps manifest and enforce a positive action plan that will bring life, hope, and purpose to one's life.

The Ezekiel method contains three essential components that guarantee successful results. These components are investigation, discovery, and natural release. It can be easily applied by utilizing the Alphabetical Building Blocks Guide for a Life Coach. The Alphabetical Building Blocks Guide for a Life Coach is a guide used to build character and awareness. When using this guide, create a sequence of questions to ask the client to touch every level within the alphabet of words provided. The terms disclosed are the most critical aspects of one's life.

Alphabetical Building Blocks Guide for a Life Coach

A- Authentic Affirmations, Application, and Accountability

B- Boldness

C- Confidence, Consistency, and Courage

D- Detox, Direction, and Development

E- Evaluate, Excel, and Expectation

F- Faithfulness and Future

G- Growth, Gratitude, and Gentleness

H- Humbleness, Humility, and Happiness

I- Identity, Integrity, Impartation, and Intentionality

J- Joy and Journey

K Knowledge and Kindness

L- Love, Life, and Liberty

M- Meekness and Movement

N- Nutrition and Newness

O- Obedience and Observation

P- Peace, Plan, and Patience

Q- Quality

R- Release, Restore, Revive, and Renew

S- Stability, Stamina, Strength and Self-Control

T- Time Management and Truth

U- Understanding

V- Virtuous, Vibrant, Value, and Victory

W- Wisdom and Willingness

X- Xenagogue and Xenas

Y- Yield

Z- Zealousness

Contact Information:

Aleshia Brown

Phone: (864) 504-4323

Email: info@empowermeministry.com

Website: empowermeministry.com

Facebook: www.Facebook.com/empowermeministry

Instagram: www.Instagram.com/empowerme_llc

How can I become better at what I do?

Chavon Anette
Partnering to Fulfill Purpose

Coaching is so much bigger than a paid job or a way to share what you know with others. Coaching is the opportunity to partner with individuals for them to get in their purpose position. Myles Monroe stated, "The fact that you are alive today is an indication that you have something the world needs." The responsibility and the opportunity that one who is called to be a coach is the chance to help individuals live out their greatest potential. Individuals benefit from the language, structure, and accountability to forge and fortify new processes and habits that will allow them to make strides and reach the goals that they have in mind for their lives. A coach has the wonderful role of helping individuals navigate the terrains of breaking cycles, glass ceilings, and limiting barriers. There are so many mindsets that are challenged and redirected in coaching. The individual comes in contact with another individual who is not only going to give strategy and accountability, but who is also one who implements the very strategies being suggested.

As a coach, I have come to love and appreciate the statement that the greatest form of leadership is self-leadership. I have been coaching since 2019. I knew that I was called to be a coach because I was the one that so many people came to for advice or wisdom. There are people who will say that certain spaces like coaching is an oversaturated market.

However, there are over 7.6 billion people in the world, and there are some people who are called to my voice and my coaching style. Also, the training that I went through was so powerful with Michelle Franklin because she focused on not only coaching others, but the essence of being able to be accountable to oneself. Therefore, as a coach, I am always being reflective of how I am showing up in the world. Leaders are always the ones that are called to go forth. A true leader will be willing to do the necessary discipline to advance and be prepared.

One key factor in being a coach is ensuring that you are able to be authentic to who you are as a coach. For me, the root of my authenticity is founded in my faith in Jesus Christ. I had to allow God to process me through some things in my alone time, so I could show up as my true, authentic self. There is power in authenticity because your focus is on the creative genius in you and what you bring to the world. Each coach brings unique history through the victories and challenges that they have faced in life. I often attribute the struggle with being authentic to almost like drowning. It is a lot of work to position yourself as you think people desire you to be rather than just being who you are. It is imperative that each coach creates from the model given and never just mimic the model given to them. There is a certain language that comes from your experiences that will reach the people that you desire to reach.

Think and consider, who are your people? What type of people need you? Authentic also means not being afraid to share your story; therefore, you must move in a way that you have embraced even the challenging seasons of your life. There will be people who come to you as a coach, but there are some areas in their lives that have been ignored or glossed over. If you have gone through the process first, you will be better able to help them and identify areas where there needs to be more attention. I am the Fire Leadership Coach. I am a faith-based leadership and life coach without apology. I share practical and spiritual tools to help women step into their purpose position and gain the language they need to surpass the goals that they set for themselves.

A second key factor is that coaches have the ability to give language to set people in position for their next level. I always say, you don't know what you don't know. A coach is able to help an individual get unstuck from seasons, mindsets, and expectations that don't speak to the potential they have on the inside of them. The coach has the ability to turn on the lights in dark areas of the unknown for the individuals that they coach to help moments of great revelation and heightened awareness. When I coach individuals, my goal is to provide language that will shift them into new belief systems and provide tools that will allow them to elevate the way they navigate life.

My coaching method is to have my clients focus on three types of goals: Destiny Goals, Career Goals, and Spiritual Goals. This approach for me speaks to the different areas where someone could need growth. It is a more wholistic approach. As a leadership and life coach, we should make the people we coach aware that all areas of our lives matter. The health and success of what anyone does will be determined by where they stand overall and not in just one place or space in their lives.

Finally, a third key is that as a coach, you will have to be innovative and intentional as it pertains to building your cliental to utilize your certification. Announcing that I became a certified leadership and life coach was exciting for me and others, but the excitement did not mean they started calling, texting, or direct messaging me to book a session. It means that they would start looking and watching me. The first thing I did was add the fact that I was a coach to my website, and then I had to figure out what would be my signature pitch as a leadership and life coach. Honestly, it has evolved over time as I worked to find my place and my voice as a leadership and life coach. Now, I call myself the Fire Leadership Coach. As I present myself as such with how I show up is what allows others to embrace me by what I uniquely offer as a coach. You have to be willing to be innovative and tap into your creative genius.

For a long time, I concluded that I was not a creative person because I had one way of looking at what creativity was. I thought creative was only someone who could design a room in a beautiful way or who was really great with artsy projects. However, being creative is so much more than that. Another definition of creative according to dictionary.com is "relating to or involving the imagination or original ideas." Therefore, as a coach, it is so important that you work to sit and create what will position you as a coach where you can serve more people. For me, I created a group coaching program. I also went on to create courses for different individuals to be able to access me and the knowledge and experience I share through a self-paced program. Never limit yourself to one-on-one coaching. Never think that a way you did things before is the way you have to do things forever. Everything can evolve as you evolve. Don't place yourself in a creative box, but it is important that you remain relevant and impact as the seasons change.

Myles Monroe- "The fact that you are alive today is an indication that you have something the world needs." My answer to the call of coaching changed me, and it also allowed me to be in position to help someone else's life also change. I believe that as a leader and a coach you are constantly going through transformation, and you have the beautiful opportunity to help others go through the transformation that you had to process through yourself.

It is a journey, and it can be uncomfortable at times, but it is one that is beautiful if you choose to stick it out. Write the vision, the mission, and the method that is unique to you, but you must always be open to allowing the creative genius in you to come alive to reach as many people as you can.

Contact Information:

Chavon Thomas
www.chavonanette.com
Power & Grace Leaders Facebook

How can I become better at what I do?

Questionnaire

Answer the questions below to help you become a better coach:

Self-Awareness

Life Skills Part (2)

Self-Awareness

It's important to get to know you and what you like. Define self-awareness and write a short paragraph about yourself.

_____

_____

_____

Empathy

Define empathy and why it's important to empathize with others?

_____

_____

_____

Compassion

Define compassion. Tell me what's the difference between empathy and compassion?

_____

_____

_____

Problem solver

Define problem solver and the role a problem solver plays in relationships. What is the job of a problem solver within relationships?

_____
_____
_____

Effective communication

How do you effectively communicate with others? Explain the dangers of poor communication within a relationship.

_____
_____
_____

Listening

Define listening and why it's important to listen in any relationship?

_____
_____
_____

What are considered cognitive skills?

_____
_____
_____

What are emotional coping skills?

_____

_____

_____

What are social skills?

_____

_____

_____

What are interpersonal skills?

_____

_____

_____

Psychology

Relationship Part (2)

Define psychology.

_____

_____

_____

How does psychology play a role person's actions?

Is learning psychology important for helping relationships?

What are the benefits of learning psychology as a relationship coach?

What are the basic principles of psychology?

What is the purpose of psychology?

Give me an example of psychology.

Is learning a person's character traits and flaws an example of psychology? Explain your answer.

Sociology

Relationship Part (3)

Define sociology.

What is one aspect of sociology?

Why does understanding sociology, better relationships?

Define human behavior from a sociology?

_____

_____

_____

Is environment a factor in human behavior?

_____

_____

_____

Made in the USA
Monee, IL
13 July 2021